The Autobiography of BRUTUS BUCKEYE

The Autobiography of BRUTUS BUCKEYE

AS TOLD TO HIS PARENTS,
SALLY LANYON AND RAY BOURHIS

ORANGE *frazer* PRESS
Wilmington, Ohio

ISBN 978-1939710-376

Orange Frazer Press
P.O. Box 214
Wilmington, OH 45177

Telephone: 937.382.3196 for price and shipping information.
Website: www.orangefrazer.com
Book and cover design: Alyson Rua and Orange Frazer Press

Library of Congress Control Number 2015948401

Photos Courtesy of:
Linda McReynolds Bryant, 63
Ray Bourhis, 63
Russ and Joan Chapman, 46, 47, 61
The Ohio State University, 1, 48–49, 50, 51, 52, 54–55, 61, 62
The Ohio State University Archives, 14, 15, 16, 18–19, 22, 23, 24–25, 26–27, 28, 30, 31, 32, 33, 34, 35, 36, 38, 39, 40, 41, 42–43, 58, 60, 61
Used with permission of *The Lantern*, the student voice of The Ohio State University, 17, 21, 26
USA TODAY Sports/Greg Bartram, 5, 8, 57, 58
USA TODAY Sports/Matthew Emmons, 53
The Columbus Dispatch, 20
Robert Flischel Photography, 12

I regret that I was unable to mention every one of my inner selves,
as you have all been so important to my story.
I love you all! —*Brutus*

This book is dedicated to all the hands and hearts that have touched or been touched by Brutus Buckeye.

Acknowledgments

The creation of a book takes the hearts and hands of a multitude of people. We are especially grateful to Marcy Hawley, Sarah Hawley, and Alyson Rua of Orange Frazer Press for believing in this project and making it vibrate on the page.

We appreciate Tamar Chute, Lisa Carter, Michelle Drobik, and Kevlin Haire from Ohio State University Archives; Nicole Kraft, Spencer Hunt, and Melanie Yutzy of *The Lantern*; and Jo McCulty of University Communications for their tremendous assistance with the many photographs they provided. We are grateful to Tony Sanfilippo of the Ohio State University Press for his expertise and advice. We thank James Barnes for his computer wizardry, Bobby Bourhis for his work with *USA Today* and other photo assistance, Michele Kern and Ivory Madison for their outstanding media assistance, and Judy Ranzer and Lynn Wiese Sneyd for their literary assistance.

Other appreciation goes to Brutus coach Raymond Sharp, Brutusmobile owners Russ and Joan Chapman, and the many people orchestrating Brutus celebration events, including Richard VanBrimmer, Tracy Stuck, Kurtis Foriska, Linda Meeks, and Barbie Tootle. We thank the organizations that have played key roles in Brutus's life—especially Ohio Staters, Block "O," Spirit Squad, Athletic Department, and Marching Band. We especially thank all the students who animated Brutus throughout the years for bringing their ideas and passion to the role.

We thank our families for their patient support. And, most of all, we thank you, Brutus, for your spirit, your character, your generosity and your devotion to OSU. No parents could be prouder than we are of you. Who could have known, back in 1965, who you, with the assistance of so many, would grow into as an adult? You are beloved, cherished and looked up to by millions as the very personification of Ohio State.

Go Bucks!
—*Sally Lanyon and Ray Bourhis*

Contents

The Autobiography of BRUTUS BUCKEYE

PART I
The Early Days

Before the Beginning

Once upon a time, believe it or not, the Ohio State Buckeyes had no mascot!

Other teams had their lions and bears, their bulldogs and steers, their boilermakers and tigers. But not OSU. From 1870 all the way until 1965—for almost a hundred years—the Ohio State Buckeyes had no Buckeye.

That was the year, 1965, that my parents, Sally Huber of Mansfield, Ohio, and Ray Bourhis of Elmhurst, New York, conceived me, changing everything forever.

Over time, stories have been told about me, legends have grown and tales have taken root, so to speak. As I move into my fiftieth year, I've been musing about how I got to this wonderful place in my life.

It all started with my parents back in 1965. Without them I wouldn't be here. I have trouble even imagining what that would be like. With no me, no Brutus. What would there be instead? Just a nothing. A void, a mascot abyss. Aaughhh! I can't even stand to think about it!

All right. So here it goes.

Meet My Parents

First, I want you to meet my parents. I love this *Makio* yearbook photo of them in Siebert Hall where they spent many hours after having met in the cafeteria between their two non-coed dorms, Siebert and Stradley Hall.

I come from good genes. Mom and Dad were both active in all kinds of campus activities. Yet they seemed to have enough time to just hang out together.

It's a Boy

Most kids in the 1960s were born in hospitals. Not me. I was born on a lawn. The crunchy autumn-leaved lawn of the Pi Beta Phi house on Indianola Avenue, just two blocks from OSU's Mershon Auditorium and the Oval.

The 1965 Homecoming game was two weeks away. Chicken wire, newspapers, and flour water goop were the tools behind the creation of floats all over campus. Enlisting the helping hands of my mom's sorority sisters, Mom and Dad molded chicken wire in the shape of a sphere over a square wooden frame. They covered all of that with papier-mâché and a few layers of paint, adding huge eyes, a big smile, and stick eyebrows to my face. After installing a strapped harness inside, I was pretty much ready to go—a grinning giant bowling ball with legs. I got my big blue eyes from my mom; my big head from my dad.

The Big Coming Out

On game day, October 30, I was moved into the bowels of the stadium before the crowds started trickling in. There I sat, hidden away until halftime.

At just the perfect moment—along with my first enthusiastic inner self—I broke through a crowd of fans and charged out onto the field, shocking the marching band and 84,359 people right out of their minds and into a bewildered screaming frenzy. What fun and such a moment! I'll never forget it. I was so happy and I could tell right away that people got it. They knew who I was, and that the days and years of the Ohio State Buckeyes being a name without a

My favorite photograph of my parents.

"We want the mascot!"

face and a team without a mascot were suddenly completely over.

Kids were screaming, grandparents were pointing, cheerleaders were cheering and fans were howling. I was launched into the world in front of a gigantic mob of adoring supporters.

It all happened so quickly, as though I'd been shot out of a cannon or something.

Then, as fast as I had come, I went. As I left, I could hear the fans screaming, "We want the mascot! We want the mascot!"

Later that afternoon, I learned that we won the Homecoming game, 11–10. A long tradition of bringing luck to the Bucks had begun.

I Get My Name

Parents are usually the ones to name their kids. Not me. Dad got Ohio Staters, Inc., to organize a campus-wide name-the-mascot contest. The Union department store offered a fifty dollar gift certificate to the first-place winner. A committee of faculty and students was set up to screen proposed names.

Kerry Reed, of Dublin, Ohio, won with the name Brutus the Buckeye. Rumor has it that other names may have had more support but that my dad favored Brutus and made sure it became my name. Some students, disgruntled because Brutus meant "heavy," or confused with *Et tu, Brute,* wanted me to be named Bucky Buckeye. How lame would that have been?

Over the years I became Brutus Buckeye, dropping my middle name. Mom still likes to call me by my full name, Brutus the Buckeye.

A New Look

I quickly went from an infant to a toddler. My papier-mâché version was kind of bulky. It was

My huge fiberglass head.

too heavy for me to be sprinting around on a one-hundred-yard stage with any kind of gusto. I learned that in my debut. I needed to lose some weight. And for sure, I wouldn't be able to travel well, having just a thin skin of newspapers held together by dried-out flour and water.

Dad paid a visit to a local fiberglass foundry. Three days later, my evolved self was delivered to Drackett Tower, ready for a coat of paint, the addition of fuzzy cotton movable eyebrows, and a grin that could be turned upside down into a frown. I could now be happy, crafty, sad, or angry.

Cool but Loud

At twenty-two pounds, a lighter, leaner, me was ready for the Dad's Day Iowa game. It was at that game that some of the marching band members started the idea of patting me on the back for good luck. Cool, but loud. Anyway, it worked against Iowa, whom we beat 38–0.

Let me explain the "loud." Fiberglass blocks out the sound of the fans, but hitting me on the shell sounded like the beating of a taiko war drum—from *inside* the drum. The other problem was that my inner self could barely see out of the two eye holes. He could look only forward and down. He could see his feet and the chalk of a sideline, but he never knew who was beside or behind him. He must have felt half blind.

My popularity was such that within weeks the Athletic Council approved me as the mascot. Not everyone agreed. People in the front rows complained that they couldn't see over me. Others didn't like the fact that I moved slowly. For crying out loud, I was just a youngster.

While the cheerleaders babysat me when I was very young, Block "O" started caring for me between games. And they did a great job, although they didn't have a stroller big enough for me, so they had to strap me to the back of a station wagon.

I had to say goodbye to my dad in 1966 and my mom in 1967. They were graduating and going on to their careers, but so was I.

17

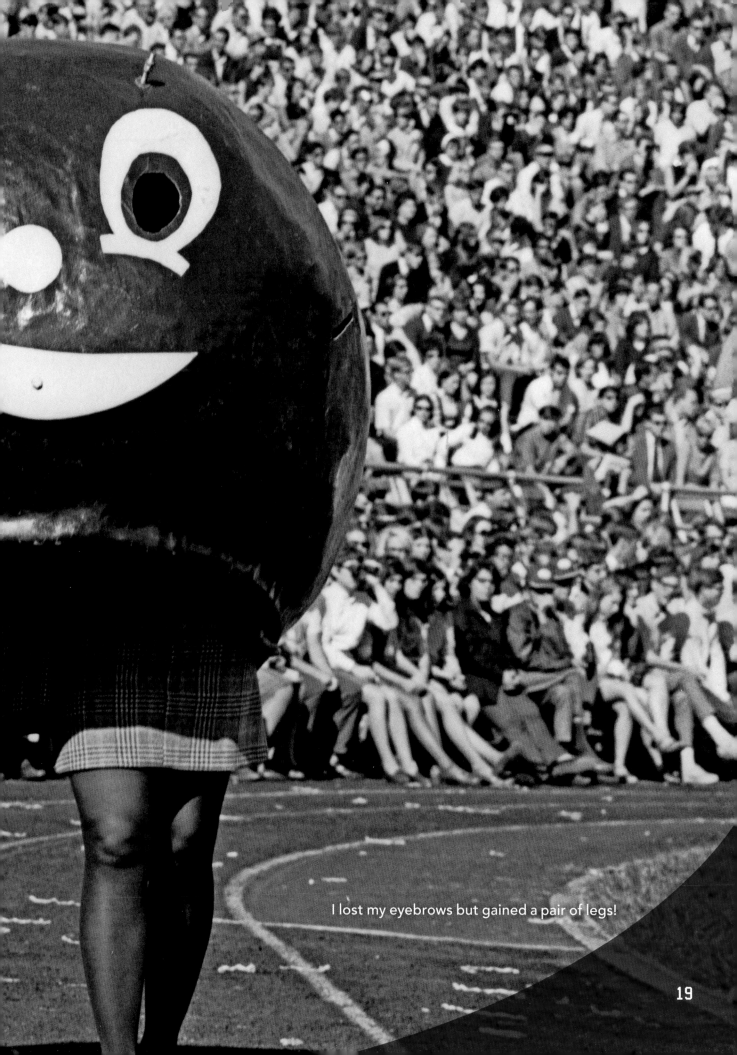

I lost my eyebrows but gained a pair of legs!

PART II
Elementary Years

Me with my inner self, Keith Burkes.

What Price Celebrity

As the spotlight widened, I became the target of mistakes and mischief. The first occurred in 1969 after the Rose Bowl. We kicked butt in Pasadena but the return to Columbus was kind of bittersweet. Somebody inadvertently left me at the Port Columbus Airport and I was, well, sort of forgotten. In twenty-degree weather, no less. Fortunately, Port Columbus employee Charles Kerecman came to the rescue. He got me a blanket, kept me nice and warm, and guarded me closely. Someone gave me big paper tears and a note taped to my forehead, "I'm lost. Please take me home."

Malicious Michigan Thugs

Although I don't really deserve much of the credit, the fact of the matter is that between 1965 and 1970, the Bucks ran up a record of 44 and 12 and beat the University of Michigan four times out of six and outscored them 118–85.

Before the OSU–Michigan game in November of 1971, I left my home in St. John Arena, traveled to Ann Arbor, and was staying with a friend. The night before the game, I was suddenly awakened by a gang of mean, nasty, U of M Theta Chi losers. They kidnapped me, beat me up, painted me with blue and yellow stripes—including my eyebrows—and dumped me the next day in the huge hole in the ground that Michigan calls its football field, right in the middle of the game. It was mortifying. I could give you more details of my incarceration but I don't want to think about it. And what was even worse, we lost the game.

Kidnapped Again?!

I was rehabbed by my friends at Block "O" with a bright new smile and rabbit fur eyebrows. Then on February 1, 1973, I was kidnapped again. By *another* group of vandals from you-know-where, I'm sure. Ann Arbor seems to have an endless supply of such folks. Again, I was beaten up. This time they dumped me in the middle of the night at the OSU Administration

...a whole new dimension

Building where I was rescued at 3:45 a.m. by the campus police.

Officer Ronald Jornd, who inspected the scene, told my Block "O" handlers and me that the kidnappers must have been very good at their task. All my protective chains were gone and no traces of cut metal could be found.

Mary Cornwell of Block "O" was overheard to say that the police had told her that the culprit was facing a possible one-year sentence with at least six months of jail time before even the possibility of parole. In my opinion, that would be too good for my captors.

Thank God for my friends at Campus Police. Once again, Block "O" handled my rehab.

Block "O" always took great care of me. I look so fresh and so clean in this picture.

I was kidnapped again in January of 1974. My captors didn't maul me this time but they hid me, raising a scare on campus. All was resolved on a happy note when my abductors, Romophos, the OSU sophomore men's honorary, inducted me into their organization in a ceremony at the January 28 basketball game.

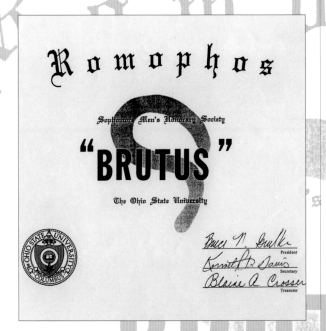

By the way, it's a good thing basketball games are played indoors. It's *cold* in Columbus in January. I was happy to go to over twenty Buckeye basketball games that year.

Friends Forever

Keith Burkes, who was from Blacklick, Ohio, was my inner self for his freshman, sophomore, and junior years. He expanded my appearances from football and basketball games

to ice hockey, baseball, track and field, swim meets, lacrosse, and soccer matches. I also appeared at programs for incoming freshmen at a barbeque hosted by President Enarson, the top guy at Ohio State. Wow. That was a real honor. Thanks to Keith, my life took on a whole new dimension. One of my favorite times with Keith was going to the Northside Nursery as part of an Ohio State United Way campaign. Adorable kids asked questions of Keith and got to pet my furry eyebrows.

Pasadena Persistence

Keith stood up for me. In December of '74, the Buckeyes were again slated to play in the Rose Bowl out in Pasadena. Somehow the university wasn't planning to send me to the game. The idea of OSU playing in such an important game without me didn't seem like a good idea— to me or to Keith. Keith threatened to hitchhike with me out to California if somebody didn't come up with the money.

This was the day Keith Burkes took me to the Northside Nursery. The kids were cute and so curious. I suppose they had never seen a gigantic buckeye before.

24

They found the money.

Keith was fabulous—so supportive and loyal. But when the cheerleaders took over my custody from Block "O" in 1974, Keith stepped aside because he didn't think he could handle the moves that the cheerleaders required. That was bittersweet for me. I was honored to be working with the fabulous OSU cheerleaders, but sad that I was no longer partnering with Keith.

It was in 1975 that Dick Otte of *The Columbus Dispatch* wrote a column calling me a homely, oversized cousin to the horse chestnut and referred to me as old hat. I wanted to say, "Hey Dick, I'll tell you who's related to a horse chestnut and who's old hat…" but I just kept quiet, which is easy for me to do.

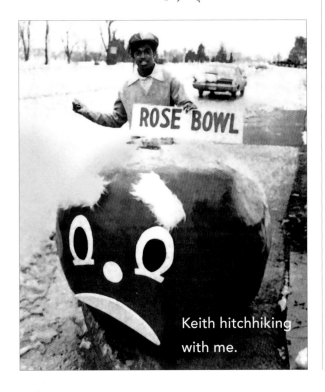

Keith hitchhiking with me.

Rose Bowl

Look at me struttin' my stuff!

PART III
Adolescence

A Valiant Attempt

As a possible result of the Dick Otte article, Jim and Sandy Hite, with, I'm sure, all good intentions, created a new Brutus persona—a sneering version with a crown and a lopsided mouth. I mean to tell you, it was *ugly*.

Fortunately, my fans came through. At the first home game at which my sneering self appeared —a game against Penn State in 1975—they booed. And I mean *booed* the ugly me right off the field chanting, "We want Brutus! We want Brutus!" YEA! Trust Ohio State fans. They always come through. When the old me reappeared at the next game, there was a cheer that could be heard in Sandusky. Dick Otte reported in *The Columbus Dispatch* an ovation that was only surpassed in duration by a triple Script Ohio. *Dick got it.*

What was good about all of this upheaval was that I knew things were getting set for the next stage in my evolution. Growth was in the wind. I could feel it in my bones. Well, in my shell.

...there was a cheer that could be heard in Sandusky.

BRUTUS BUCKEYE

JAMES HITE 7-14-75

Sneering Brutus got the boot. He looked too mean and was not cute. Not at all.

Archie Griffin, the nicest Buckeye around.

Attempting our Heisman pose.

Archie

The best thing I remember about 1975 was Archie Griffin. What a guy he was and is. Woody Hayes's famous statement about Archie was that, "He's a better young man than he is a football player, and he's the best football player I've ever seen."

Archie's history at Ohio State started in 1972, as a freshman. In his first game he set a school record,

rushing for 239 yards. Over the next four years, he led the Bucks to four Big Ten Championships and four Rose Bowls. In 1974, he won the famous Heisman Trophy—as a junior. Then in 1975, he won it again. Unbelievable! And unmatched!

Over the years I have tried to emulate Archie's quiet reserve and kindness for his fans, patiently taking time for photos and autographs. Neither of us says much. Our actions speak for themselves.

From Mean to Mousey

After the snarling Brutus fiasco, I went back to my former self, and then I evolved once again in 1977. I lost my white eyebrows to short black ones forever poised in a worried, up-tilted position. I looked kind of cute, I guess, in a mousey sort of way. But I gained too much weight. I zoomed up to 80 pounds. This was no easy task for Sandy Foreman, my first coed inner self, but she handled it like a pro. And because my head could be taken apart, I could travel to more away games than before!

This version of me gave me a complex. I looked too worried.

Lenny Shutzberg and I taking a breather. It was a lot of work being an energetic nut!

My inner self in 1979 and 1980 was Lenny Shutzberg. In those days two things were different from now. First, it was okay for people to know who my inner self was; second, I was the consolation prize at cheerleader tryouts. The CONSOLATION prize. What a horrible idea. Lenny agreed with me, and he set out to change all of that.

Here's how it happened. Pre-Lenny, they had cheerleader tryouts once a year. Those who came out performed cartwheels, flips, and so on. They selected however many cheerleaders they needed, and then the one who came in next became my inner self. In other words, the one who didn't quite make the cut as a cheerleader got the consolation prize—me. Is that dumb or what? Dumb and insulting.

Well, Lenny didn't want to be a cheerleader. He wanted to be *me*. But given the system, he had to go through the motions. He landed on his head in a handspring, and in a lift, he dropped a girl. He didn't make the cut. But then he went to Richard Delaney, OSU's Assistant Athletic Director, to try and sell him on two things—one, that he should become my next inner self and two, that a whole new protocol should be established for future Brutus tryouts based on personality and enthusiasm, not based on also-ran flipping skills. Lenny won on both counts.

I sure miss my mentor, Richard Delaney.

My Mentor

In addition to Archie, the most important force behind my career was a mentor who believed in me and shaped me into who I am today. That mentor was Richard Delaney, whose vision and determination prepared me for the national spotlight. Richard served as assistant athletic director, then associate director. He was a force behind so many of the wonderful things that occurred in my evolution, up until his untimely death to cancer in 1985.

In 1980, Richard announced that he had been working on a secret project for three years. It was top secret, like the Manhattan Project.

Finally in September 1981, Richard let the cat out of the bag. His project was revealed. It was a makeover. I had a smaller head, arms, and my tan spot was moved from the top of my head to my face. Richard's work gave me a whole new sense of myself. In addition to the new look, the new me allowed my personality to come out. I had big clown feet, white striped socks, and gloves on my hands. Very cool.

Angel versus Devil

Forty-five students tried out to animate me that year. I guess I was getting really popular! The newly formed Brutus judging panel ranked candidates by their enthusiasm, creativity, and showmanship, to match my effervescent personality. And guess who won? A coed! Not just any coed, but an angel! Mary Burnett of Bryan, Ohio. I was launched at the home game against Duke. And it was very symbolic. An Angel versus a Blue Devil.

Mary was terrific. What an attitude! She made me more fan-friendly than ever before. She taught me to shake hands and interact with fans and to sign autographs.

The Spangler Candy Company of Bryan, Ohio, gave her a thousand red lollipops to hand out and Mary danced around and did cheers. It was a great year.

Here I am in a dress and striped stockings!

PART IV
The Modern Me

Darwin was Right

I kept evolving. And in 1982 Eric Mayer, a sophomore from Beachwood, Ohio, added slacks, a striped football jersey with 00 on the front, and tennis shoes. Eric was quoted by Don Baird of *The Columbus Dispatch* as saying that he wanted to add gymnastics into my routine. Let me tell you that although tumbling was easy, learning more sophisticated gymnastics was a challenge.

In addition to the gymnastics, Eric let me run around Ohio Stadium pumping up our fans and shaking my fist at opponents. Boy, did I ever love that. Sometimes the other side would get really sensitive and touchy about it. But the more sensitive and touchy I could get them to be, the better I liked it.

Our fans loved it. I learned to whip them into an almost frenzy. Laughing, screaming, squealing with joy, and bursting with energy.

Roller Coaster

In 1984, I was kidnapped again. This time, right out of Eric Mayer's car. As usual, the criminals were a handful of disgruntled malcontents. WSNY-FM offered a $500 reward and GTE Telsystems added $1,000 plus the use of a helicopter if I was found outside the state. But before things got completely out of hand, a man by the name of Frankie Alexander contacted OSU News Director Dave Garick with the good news that while searching for aluminum cans, he had found me in a dumpster. No helicopter was necessary.

In November 1984, for *the* Game, I showed the scarlet and gray in my veins by donating blood to the Central Ohio Red Cross Center. It was all part of the annual blood drive contest between the Buckeyes and The Team Up North that bleeds blue and yellow.

Then, uh oh, in the summer of 1985, Eric was ticketed for jaywalking. Jaywalking? You can't walk anywhere in Columbus without jaywalking! It's like getting a ticket for not wearing a seat belt on a bicycle. Nevertheless, AP and UPI picked up the story, showing how visible you are in Eric's position. It's a good thing he wasn't busted for anything else! It would have made the NBC Nightly News.

A photo of me trying to get students excited at a pep rally.
It was much easier to jump around with a smaller head.

Enter Scott Geyer

Since the age of six, Scott Geyer, of Springfield, Ohio, had dreamed of playing football for Woody Hayes. When he finally got to OSU, he decided to turn his attention to me.

In a statement to *The Lantern* in 1986, Scott said I had become the personification of the whole university—the very symbol of OSU. Among many other things, Scott taught me to run out of the tunnel with the team at the start of every game. What a rush! The fans would go nuts (Get it?). The energy was incredible.

Brutus the Bankroller

I continued making numerous additional personal appearances at university-sponsored or approved events. Then, in September of 1987, I even got my own trademark symbol. Complete with clenched fists, muscles, and a determined look on my face, I was described by Ruth Hanley of *The Columbus Dispatch* as a "lean, mean, athletic machine."

The university soon starting selling things with my image on them: stuffed animals, tee shirts, hats, key chains, calendars, you name it.

All of this produced real revenue. Pretty soon I was bringing in hundreds of thousands of dollars a year for student aid. This amounted to dozens of grants per year to scores of deserving students. Brutus the Bankroller! I tried smoking big cigars for promo shots, but they made me sick.

Speaking of Promos

Later in '87, I did a soft shoe dance with Doctors Hospital interns at their ninth annual on-stage performance at the Ohio Theatre. Nobody knew it, but I had practiced for weeks and I have to say I think I did a pretty good job. A woman ran up to me afterward to ask for an autograph. She said I reminded her of Fred Astaire.

Two Inner Selves

By 1990, I was so busy I had two inner selves, Bart Suver and Doug Congrove.

In October 1991, I dressed up as a ghost for the Michigan State game. That was a kick, but when I looked in the mirror I scared myself half to death. Freaky! I decided right then and there no more ghosts.

At the Hall of Fame Bowl in Tampa in 1992, I worked on getting rid of my winter Ohio pallor. An aluminum foil reflector did the trick! No sunscreen, no Coppertone, no floppy-brimmed hat, no nothing.

Makes My Heart Beat

Given all the fun and frolic, my favorite activity has been visiting with patients and visitors at Ohio State's University Hospital. I have to say that visiting hospitals—especially visiting children in hospitals—is one of the most rewarding things I do. Sometimes they are kids who have suffered burns. Other times they've been in horrible accidents. No matter how bad off they are, or how tired or scared because of just being where they are, never once have I encountered one of these young people who didn't drop whatever she or he was doing and break into a big grin when I walked into the room. To be able to do that feels like something I could never put into words or explain. I'm glad they couldn't see the tears running down the faces of my inner selves.

Music

As everybody knows I LOVE music. All kinds of music. Classical, rock, show songs, and of course, my favorite—marching band music. I think of it as a kind of universal language. And so, in 1993 when, along with the marching band, I went to the Columbus Symphony's closing Summer Pops concert, it was really something. It was a beautiful experience. For a moment, the thought crossed my mind that maybe I was going to run into the same lady that had said I reminded her of Fred Astaire back at the '87 Doctors Hospital soft shoe event, but it didn't happen. In any event, the Pops concert was fabulous. I decided right then and there to go to more concerts as soon and as often as possible.

The pairing continued. In 1995, it was Mario Nedelkoski and Mike Braun. At about that time my inner selves became anonymous, and they adopted a kind of vow of silence. Like monks.

Jamie Cleverley took over for Mike. And Jamie and Mario were really terrific. Both of them let me go a little crazy sometimes leading cheers, running all over the stadium, tweaking the other mascots. I especially loved tweaking the Michigan State Spartan. He takes himself so seriously.

But I'll tell you who I would really love to tweak.

I would REALLY love to tweak U of M's Wolverine mascot. But—can you believe it—they don't have one. No mascot up there in Ann Arbor. Maybe that's why they keep trying to steal me!

Brutusmobile

In 2003 Russ Chapman of Ashland, Ohio, launched his Brutusmobile. A spectacular candy apple red and gray 1929 Model A Ford Deluxe Roadster named after me! It has a Woody Hayes hood ornament, a Brutus gear shift, Block "O" turn signals, an oak trunk, and a musical horn that plays the OSU fight song. It has been in the homecoming parade every year since 2003 and was featured in an HBO television documentary on the Ohio State–Michigan rivalry.

I have to say that in my opinion, the Brutusmobile beats out every other theme-sake mobile car in the world, including the Popemobile housed over in Vatican City, Italy. The Popemobile is very nice but it doesn't play any Gregorian chants or Christmas carols and doesn't have anybody special—if you know what I'm talking about—displayed as a hood ornament or gear shift knob.

My parents, Sally Lanyon and Ray Bourhis.

Big Reunion

A big year for me was 2006. I hadn't seen my parents for years. When the president of Ohio State, Karen Holbrook, called my dad to invite him and my mom back to Columbus for a reunion with me, I was thrilled. The university loved me so much the Homecoming theme was "Where's Brutus?"

When Mom and Dad arrived, I didn't get to see them right away because they were scooted off to ride in the rumble seat of the Brutusmobile in the Homecoming Parade. Well, as luck would have it, Columbus had the biggest rainstorm in memory, right in the middle of the parade. I mean, it was a soggy day in Brutusville. And a rumble seat in a rainstorm is not a very dry place to be. Not even with umbrellas. By the time I met up with them at the Pep Rally in the Student Union, they were wetter than a pair of gulf shrimps in a Louisiana bayou. They were soaked but happy as could be to see me.

My Extended Family

Since then, we have had several get-togethers, including one a few years later at which I met for the first time my stepbrother, Matthew.

I got my dance skills from my mom, Sally!

...cheering them on

Later this year I'm looking forward to getting together with all my siblings: Bobby, Andrew, Danielle, and Matthew Bourhis and Tom and Brian Markworth.

Hall of Famer

By 2007, I was making appearances on behalf of the Cystic Fibrosis Foundation—Great Strides—Race for the Cure, the Make-A-Wish Foundation, and many other such organizations. In addition, I was having fun showing up on ESPN, ABC Sports, *Jeopardy*, and *The Daily Show with Jon Stewart*. Then, suddenly—and I couldn't believe this—I was nominated and inducted into the Mascot Hall of Fame. That was the same year that, with yours truly cheering them on, our basketball team, under head coach Thad Matta, made it to the Final Four.

I can always count on my cheerleaders for support!

A True Test

By 2008, I got in the habit of celebrating Buckeye touchdowns by doing a push-up per point. This seemed like a good idea when we scored twenty or thirty or even forty points, but to test my resolve (and my physical shape) in 2010 the Bucks scored 73 points in a game against Eastern Michigan (the most points scored by the Buckeyes since 1950 when they beat Iowa, 83–21). "Okay, fine," I thought. "If you guys can break your record for points scored, I can bloody well do the same for my previous record for push-ups," which was forty-seven. So I did. Seventy-three push-ups, right there on the football field. Up down, up down, up down, up down. It seemed to take forever. The aches and pains and burning muscles were horrific. My arms will never be the same. But I did it. And the fans loved it. I'm not a betting kind of guy, but if I were, I could have made a fortune right then and there. Nobody thought I would be able to do it.

From 2005 through 2009, we landed five Big Ten championships (two of them outright) and played in five bowl games, including two for the national championship. *Boom Boom Boom.* One right after the other. I really built up my biceps!

Hold That Pose

In 2008, there were 250 mini-me's around Columbus in a public art show entitled "Brutus on Parade." It was more fun than the cow roundup in Chicago or the ponies in Tucson. My favorite statue was of our very own President Gordon Gee. The funds raised from "Brutus on Parade"

He ain't heavy, he's my brother!

Boom Boom Boom.

went for a very good cause, the William Oxley Thompson Memorial Library renovation.

When the new Student Union was opened in 2010, one of the main photo op attractions was right there in the center, a bronze sculpture of yours truly.

On November 28, 2011, Urban Meyer signed up to coach the Buckeyes. Three years later, they were ready.

The year 2014 was the very first year that the NCAA used a playoff system to determine the national college football champion. The Bucks had been ranked pretty high in the preseason. We had a quarterback, Braxton Miller, who was a Heisman Trophy candidate. But then Braxton was injured before the first game and was out for the season. And so J.T. Barrett, our second-string quarterback, took over. After a surprising loss to

Everyone should get to rush onto a football field at least once in their lifetime.

53

win after win

Virginia Tech, our ranking fell and most pundits wrote us off as even a long shot contender for one of the final four slots that would play for the national championship.

Not me. Not Urban Meyer. And not my Bucks.

J.T. Barrett proceeded to rack up win after win after win. Nine games in a row. Then, in the tenth game, in the process of trouncing Michigan 42–28, the unthinkable happened: J.T. broke his ankle. Our second starting quarterback of the year was o-u-t, out. We were now down to our third-string quarterback, Cardale Jones. Fans scrambled to find out who he was. Jones had never started a college football game in his life. His first start would be against Wisconsin for the Big 10 Championship with a possible berth in the national championship quartet riding along in the process. Could he do it?

The answer to that question will live in the annals of Ohio State history forever.

The score was OSU 59–Wisconsin 0.

Jones gave a new meaning to the word "magnificent." His passes were perfect. His runs were incredible. Ohio State—along with Alabama, Florida State, and Oregon—was going to be playing for the national championship.

Good Morning America

The next thing I knew, I was appearing on *Good Morning America*.

Think about it. A mascot that couldn't talk featured on one of the biggest talk shows in America! What a riot! At least I couldn't say the wrong thing. Right?

Back to the tournament. Oregon defeated Florida State in the semifinals, and we did the same to Alabama.

So there we were. With one game left in, arguably, the most exciting football season ever. The game was short and sweet. Oregon, a fabulous powerful team, put up a hard fight, but the final score was Buckeyes 42–Oregon 20.

We won! We won the National Championship!

Another really heavy dose of Brutus publicity promptly commenced.

THE Trophy

Coach Meyer and his incredible team let me actually hold the trophy. And I must say, it brought a tear to my eye just to touch it.

Sweet victory!

NATIONAL CHAMPIONSHIP

57

Summer's heat or winter cold, the seasons pass the years will roll. Time and change will surely show How firm thy friendship...Ohio.

Postscript

I'm a simple being. I'm not married. I wear the same things every day: my red and gray long sleeved shirt, red pants, white wrist bands, socks, and towel, gloves, high-topped sneakers, and my Woody Hayes baseball cap. I go to work on time. I enjoy what I do. I'm not going to move. I try to keep up with the times. I even tweet.

I've seen a lot of changes in the past fifty years. Women, who in 1965 were a rarity in law, medicine, and MBA programs, now constitute a majority in many graduate schools. Friends who used to have to wait in line to use a dorm or Greek house phone can now call or text their friends instantly. Research that had to be done manually is now available with a touch on an iPad. There are no more curfews. Cars are all but gone and bikes are everywhere. The wars against race, gender, sexuality, and other discriminations are steadily being won. The times, they are a-changin'.

But what's still the same are the Orton Hall chimes, students lounging on the oval, the quiet magic of Mirror Lake during a snowfall, the marching band playing "Hang on Sloopy," William Oxley Thompson standing steady in the middle of it all, and the ringing words of our alma mater:

Summer's heat or winter's cold, the seasons pass the years will roll. Time and change will surely show. How firm thy friendship…OHIO.

In the last analysis, in addition to its undisputed, extraordinary success in athletics, the best things Ohio State stands for, to me, are not just seen on its football, lacrosse, and soccer fields; its ice hockey rinks, swimming pools, or baseball diamonds; or its basketball, tennis, or gymnastics courts. They are also seen in OSU's classrooms, laboratories, and research facilities where round-the-clock efforts are constantly in progress, aimed at educating and serving humanity and making the world a healthier, safer, and better place.

It is in that context that I am so proud to be playing a role in the spirit of what Ohio State is all about. I love being the face of Ohio State, a part of this incredible, fabulous university.

Thank you all so much.
GO BUCKS!

Love, Brutus

Brutus, in a nutshell...

1965

1974

1975

1977

Papier-mâché Brutus is born and is soon followed by a new, fiberglass version.

Brutus appears at the Rose Bowl in Pasadena, California.

A grouchier Brutus makes an entrance, but is quickly superseded by his fiberglass counterpart.

A mousey Brutus with a big hat takes the stage.

1981   2003   2007   2015

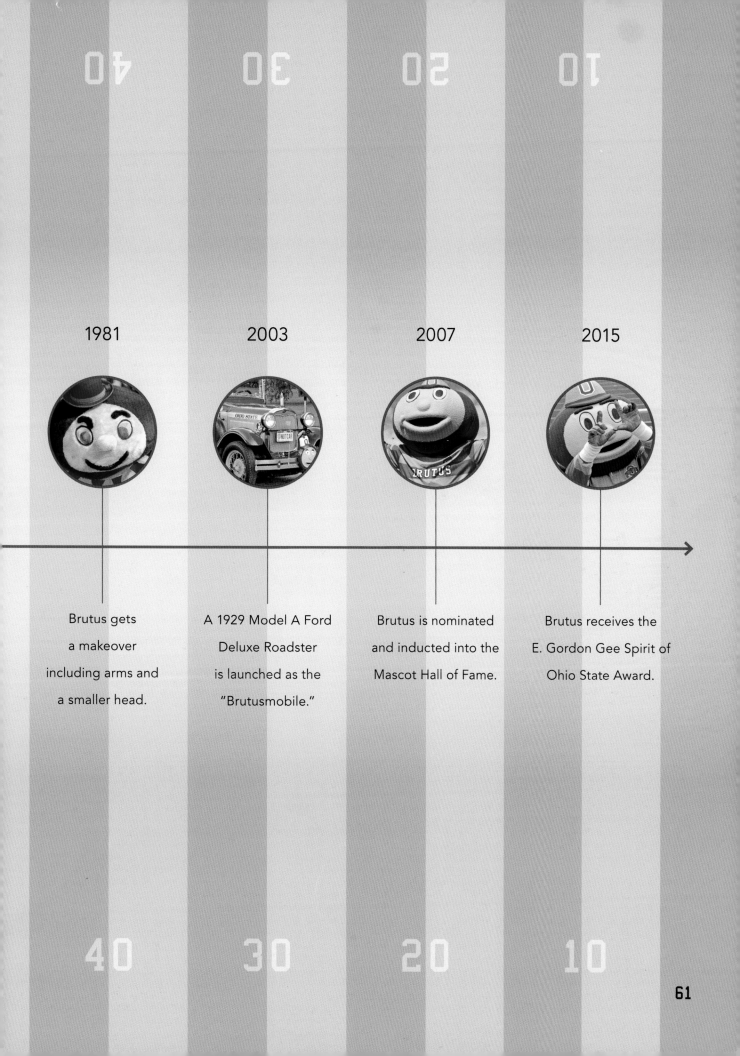

Brutus gets
a makeover
including arms and
a smaller head.

A 1929 Model A Ford
Deluxe Roadster
is launched as the
"Brutusmobile."

Brutus is nominated
and inducted into the
Mascot Hall of Fame.

Brutus receives the
E. Gordon Gee Spirit of
Ohio State Award.

About My Parents

Ray Bourhis is a lawyer in San Francisco and Santa Barbara, California, specializing in representing physicians in long-term disability insurance matters. He is a graduate of The Ohio State University and UC Berkeley School of Law.

At Ohio State, he co-founded the Pre-Law Club, served as an associate justice on the student court, designed and installed the fountain in Mirror Lake, and fathered Brutus the Buckeye. He was a member of Ohio Staters, Inc., and Block "O."

In addition to *Autobiography of Brutus Buckeye*, he is the author of *Insult to Injury: Insurance, Fraud and the Big Business of Bad Faith* and *Billionaires and Bagmen: Now What?*

The father of four children, he lives in Montecito, California.

Sally Lanyon (nee Huber) is an Organizational Development Consultant and Six Sigma Black Belt from Tucson, Arizona, with a career in healthcare and aerospace. She is a graduate of The Ohio State University and University of Arizona.

At Ohio State, she co-founded and served as president of the Pre-Law Club, sat on the Arts College Council, was an Ohio State chapter officer of the Intercollegiate Association of Women Students, and mothered Brutus the Buckeye. She gave the Student Response speech at the March 16, 1967, graduation.

She co-authored *Life after Loss: A Group for the Bereaved* (out of print) during her tenure as a hospice bereavement counselor.

She is the mother and step-mother of four children and has seven grandchildren.